DIGESTIVE SYSTEM

Priyanka Lamichhane

Children's Press®
An imprint of Scholastic Inc.

Content Consultant
Darlene Negbenebor, MD
Stamford Gastroenterology

Dedication: To my parents, Chinta and Lalita Lamichhane, who always show us unconditional love.
—Priyanka Lamichhane

Library of Congress Cataloging-in-Publication Data available
ISBN 978-1-339-02102-7 (library binding) | ISBN 978-1-339-02103-4 (paperback)

10 9 8 7 6 5 4 3 2 1   24 25 26 27 28

Printed in China 62
First edition, 2024

Design by Kathleen Petelinsek
Series produced by Spooky Cheetah Press

Find the Truth!

Everything you are about to read is true *except* for one of the sentences on this page.

Which one is **TRUE**?

T or F Rumbling is our stomach's way of telling us we're hungry.

T or F The small intestine is longer than the large intestine.

Find the answers in this book.

What's in This Book?

Your digestive
system turns
food into fuel
for your body!

4

Your tongue has lots of taste buds!

The **BIG** Truth

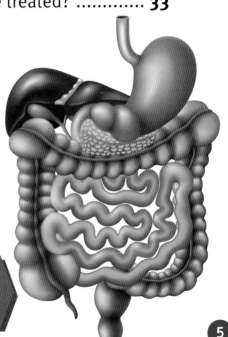

This is what part of your digestive system looks like.

INTRODUCTION

Have you ever wondered what happens to a glass of milk after you drink it—or what happens to an orange or a sandwich after you take a bite? **Food is the fuel** your body needs to keep running. But before food can be used for fuel, it has to be **converted** into the **nutrients** your body needs. That is the job of your **digestive system**. Your digestive system is made up of the **upper** and **lower** digestive tracts, as well as accessory **organs**. And each has an important role to play. Read on to learn more about this remarkable process!

Eating oranges can give your body an energy boost.

It takes our bodies an average of 2 days to fully digest food and get rid of it when we use the bathroom.

Fruit has important nutrients your body needs.

Your digestive system does not rely on gravity. Food will still go down even if you are standing on your head!

1

Where It All Begins

You may be surprised to learn that digestion really does begin in your mouth. That is the start of your upper digestive tract. That's also where most of your taste buds are found—those little organs that make the first steps of digestion so yummy. Your epiglottis [ep-uh-GLAH-tuhs], esophagus [i-SAH-fuh-guhs], and stomach are also part of the upper digestive tract.

Chomp, Chomp

The digestion of solid foods starts with our teeth. Liquids bypass this part of the process. We have different types of teeth, and each serves a different purpose. Incisors are the four front top and bottom teeth. They help with biting and cutting food. Canine teeth are on either side of the incisors. They are pointy and are used for tearing food. Next, we have premolars. They help us crush and grind food. Finally, the molars help us chew food into smaller pieces.

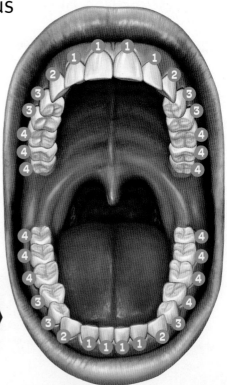

1 Incisors
2 Canine
3 Premolars
4 Molars

Most adults have 32 teeth (pictured). Kids have 20. They are called baby teeth.

Without saliva you wouldn't be able to taste dry food!

Super Saliva

Your teeth aren't working alone while you're chewing your food. As soon as you take your first bite, glands in your mouth start making saliva. The saliva contains **enzymes** that help break down food. When necessary, saliva also helps make food moist so it will be easier to swallow.

11

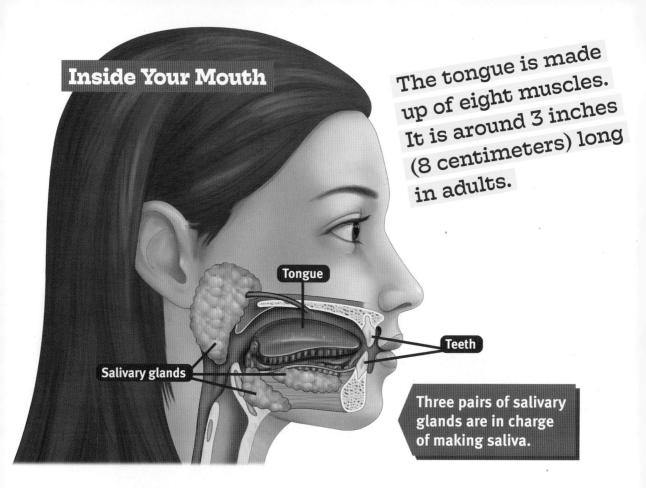

The tongue is made up of eight muscles. It is around 3 inches (8 centimeters) long in adults.

Tongue

Teeth

Salivary glands

Three pairs of salivary glands are in charge of making saliva.

The Terrific Tongue

Your tongue also plays a part in breaking down food by mixing it with saliva as you chew. As the food turns to mush, the tongue moves it to the back of the mouth. Then it pushes the food to the throat. Once the food—or drink—reaches the throat, your swallowing **reflex** is triggered.

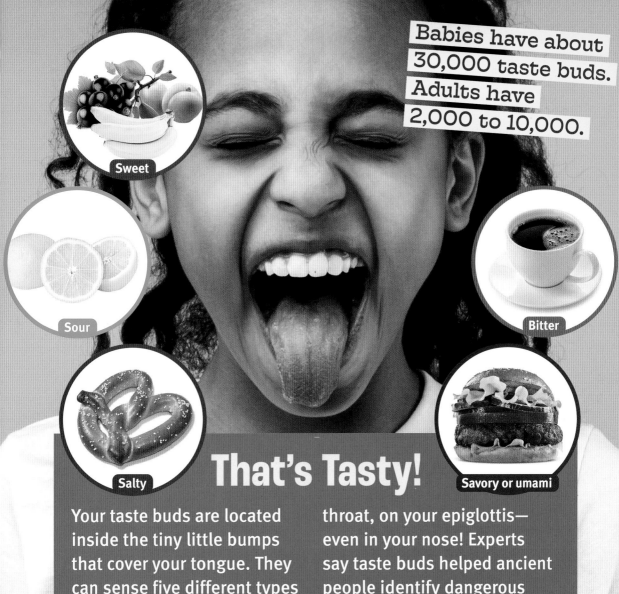

Sweet

Sour

Bitter

Salty

Savory or umami

That's Tasty!

Your taste buds are located inside the tiny little bumps that cover your tongue. They can sense five different types of flavors: sweet, sour, salty, bitter, and savory—also called umami [oo-MAH-mee]. But taste buds aren't just located on the tongue. There are taste buds in the back of your throat, on your epiglottis—even in your nose! Experts say taste buds helped ancient people identify dangerous foods. Unsafe foods tasted bitter or sour. Foods that tasted salty or sweet were safe to eat. Today our taste buds help us enjoy our food, but our lives don't depend on them!

The Router

The epiglottis is a tiny flap at the base of the tongue. When you are not eating, the epiglottis is upright, allowing air to pass through your trachea [TRAY-kee-uh] to your lungs. When you swallow, the epiglottis falls back to cover the opening of your trachea to prevent food and fluid from passing to the lungs. This keeps you from choking and allows your food or drink to continue its route through your digestive system.

The epiglottis is made of cartilage, the same stuff as the outside of your ears and nose.

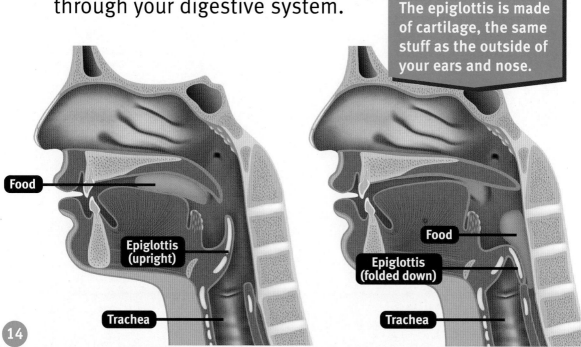

Food

Epiglottis (upright)

Trachea

Food

Epiglottis (folded down)

Trachea

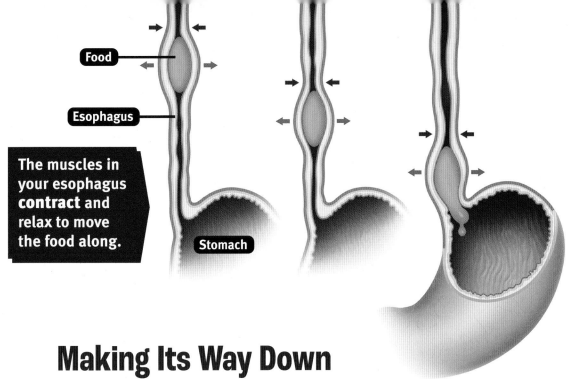

Food

Esophagus

The muscles in your esophagus **contract** and relax to move the food along.

Stomach

Making Its Way Down

Next, your food moves through a circular muscle called a sphincter. It opens to let food pass into the esophagus—which is a hollow, muscular tube that connects to your stomach. The esophagus produces a slimy substance as its muscles push the food down. There is another sphincter muscle at the bottom of the esophagus. It opens and your food continues on its journey.

You also have sphincter muscles in your eyes. They make your pupils get bigger and smaller.

The Super Stomach

Your stomach is located in the upper part of your **abdomen**. It is like a stretchy sac. It can expand as it fills up. When food enters your stomach, glands release juices made of enzymes and acids. That helps to mix the food. The juices also kill harmful **bacteria** that may be in your food. Those acids are very strong. That is why the lining of the stomach is covered with mucus. Without this mucus the stomach would digest itself!

An empty stomach is about 12 inches (30.5 cm) long and six inches (15 cm) across at its widest point. That is a little bigger than a football.

Some of the acids in the stomach are strong enough to dissolve metal!

Mix It Up . . . and Release!

At the same time your stomach juices are digesting food, your stomach is also expanding and contracting. This process is called churning. It mixes up food and turns it into a soupy substance called chyme [KIME]. The muscles at the bottom of the stomach relax to release the chyme into the small intestine a little bit at a time. If you eat a large meal, it can take the stomach about four hours to empty itself of all of the food.

It takes about 20 minutes for your brain to realize your stomach is full.

Exercises that raise your heart rate help keep your digestive system healthy.

It's best to wait at least three hours after eating a meal before you exercise.

2

We Need Nutrients

During the digestive process, nutrients are **absorbed** by our bodies. That begins to happen once chyme enters your small intestine in the lower digestive tract. Your small intestine is where most of the nutrients from our food are absorbed and sent throughout the body. These nutrients give us energy, help us grow, repair cells, and keep us healthy.

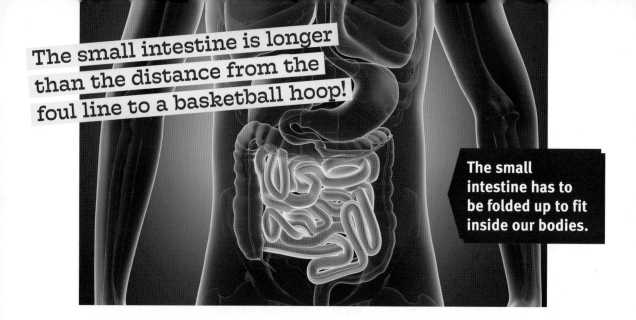

The small intestine is longer than the distance from the foul line to a basketball hoop!

The small intestine has to be folded up to fit inside our bodies.

Not So Small After All

The small intestine is about one inch (2.5 cm) around. It is also about 20 feet (6 meters) long, making it the longest part of our digestive system. The small intestine is made up of three parts. The first section, which is right below the stomach, is called the duodenum [doo-ah-DEE-nuhm]. It's shaped like the letter C. Next comes the jejunum [jih-JOO-nuhm]. The last—and longest—part of the small intestine is the ileum [IH-lee-uhm]. It is almost 10 feet (3 m) long.

Help From Friends

Several of our other organs help the small intestine do its job. The liver makes a liquid called bile and the pancreas [PAN-kree-uhs] makes enzymes. In between meals, bile is stored in the gallbladder. During a meal, bile flows to the duodenum. There it mixes with the chyme and with enzymes from the pancreas. Bile breaks down some fats in the chyme. The enzymes break down proteins, carbohydrates, and other fats. Most, but not all, nutrients are absorbed in the jejunum.

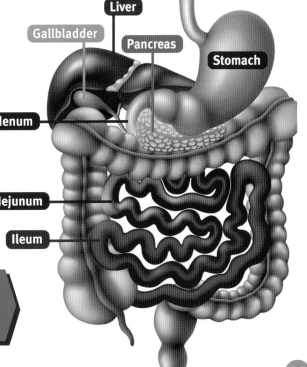

Many organs in our body work together to digest our food.

Taking It All In

The walls of the small intestine are lined with millions of tiny fingerlike structures called villi [VIL-eye]. Digestive enzymes in the villi break nutrients down into even smaller pieces. Then **blood vessels** in the villi carry nutrients to the liver, where they are processed to be usable by the body. It takes 4 to 6 hours for food to be digested in the small intestine. What is left moves on to the next part of the process. That includes fiber, which is the parts of plant foods that our bodies cannot digest.

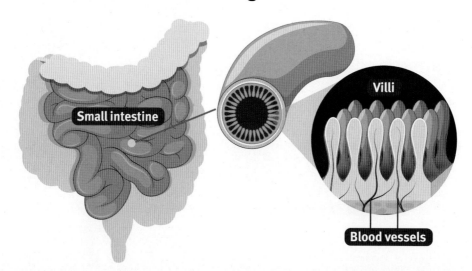

Small intestine

Villi

Blood vessels

Fiber keeps our digestive system healthy. Among other things, it helps our bodies get rid of waste.

Many Nutrients

Our bodies need different kinds of nutrients to function properly. Nutrients are divided into two main groups: macronutrients and micronutrients. Carbohydrates, proteins, and fats are macronutrients. Our bodies need lots of them to give us energy. Foods like fruits and whole-grain breads and pastas are good sources of carbohydrates. Proteins help build and repair tissues in our bodies. They are found in meat, fish, beans, and eggs. Fats give us energy and help protect our organs. Oils, nuts, and butter are three foods that contain fats. Vitamins and minerals are micronutrients. Our bodies need them only in very small amounts. They help our bodies work properly, build our bones, and strengthen our **immune system**. Fruits, vegetables, and dairy products are rich in micronutrients.

Washing your hands after using the bathroom helps keep you safe from germs.

It takes about 36 hours for food to go through the large intestine.

3

Making Its Way Out

After our bodies absorb nutrients from the food we eat, undigested food, or waste, is left. This waste needs to leave our bodies. The large intestine is the part of the lower digestive tract where this process begins. The large intestine is about 5 feet (1.5 m) long and 3 inches (8 cm) wide and is attached to the end of your small intestine at the cecum [SEE-kum]. The large intestine is also known as the colon.

Large and in Charge

When the cecum is full, the muscles in the colon start contracting to move the waste along. The large intestine is home to more than 1,000 types of bacteria, both healthy and unhealthy, that live in balance with one another. The good bacteria help prevent the growth of harmful bacteria. They also help break down fiber.

Parts of the Large Intestine

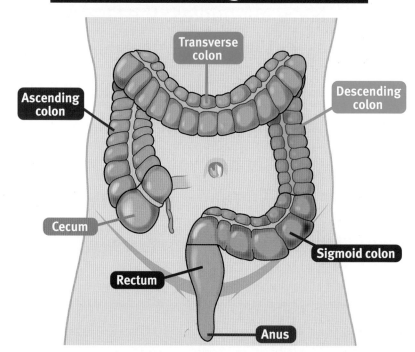

Transverse colon

Ascending colon

Descending colon

Cecum

Sigmoid colon

Rectum

Anus

It's a Mystery

The appendix is a small tubelike tissue attached to the cecum. It is 2 to 4 inches (5 to 10 cm) long. Scientists are not sure what the appendix does. They think it might store healthy bacteria to help the digestive and immune systems. For example, if the balance of good bacteria in the intestines is off, the appendix might send out more good bacteria to keep the intestines healthy.

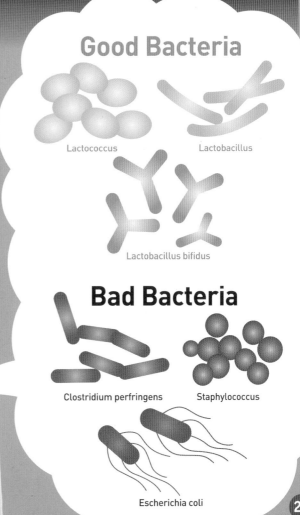

Good Bacteria

Lactococcus

Lactobacillus

Lactobacillus bifidus

Bad Bacteria

Clostridium perfringens

Staphylococcus

Escherichia coli

Appendix

27

Absorbing Water

The large intestine is also in charge of absorbing water from the undigested waste as it makes its way through. This happens in the ascending colon. The water passes through the walls of the colon into the bloodstream. Removing water from the waste makes it more solid. But not all water is absorbed. Any additional water comes out with the waste when you go to the bathroom. In addition to undigested food and water, the waste also contains dead cells and mucus.

Timeline: The Digestive Process*

MINUTE 1:
Your food goes into the mouth and is swallowed.

5 to 8 SECONDS later:
Your food goes through the esophagus and into the stomach.

2 to 6 HOURS after entering the stomach: The food is now chyme. At this point, your stomach drops chyme into the small intestine every 20 seconds. How long this process takes depends on how much you have eaten, among other things.

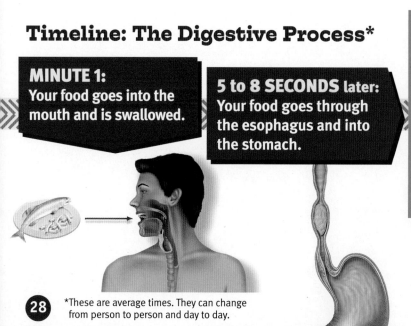

*These are average times. They can change from person to person and day to day.

The Rectum

The rectum is the last 5–6 inches (10–15 cm) of the large intestine. That is where waste is held until you go to the bathroom. Nerves in the rectum sense when it is full. They send a message to the brain that it is time to go to the bathroom. Then the brain tells the muscles in the rectum to let the waste out. The poop makes its way out through the very end of the rectum, an opening called the anus.

Poop is mostly water.

5 HOURS after entering the small intestine: The chyme has gone through the small intestine, and nutrients have been absorbed. The waste makes its way to the cecum, the sac at the start of the large intestine.

ABOUT 36 HOURS after entering the large intestine: Waste has made its way through the large intestine and now it is in the rectum, ready to come out.

ABOUT 2 DAYS after food entered the mouth: The food has gone through the entire digestive process and waste is exiting the body.

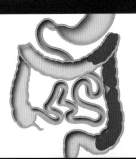
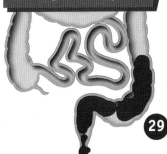

Teamwork!

The digestive system supplies all of your body systems with the nutrients they need to work properly. In turn, the different systems help your digestive system in many ways:

Circulatory System: →

After nutrients are absorbed by the small intestine and processed by the liver, the circulatory system carries them throughout the body. The circulatory system also provides your digestive system with the oxygen-rich blood it needs to work.

Muscular System:

Your tongue is a muscle. Other muscles in the throat, stomach, and intestines contract and relax to carry food on its long journey through your body.

Circulatory System

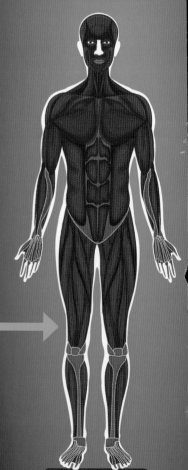

Muscular System

Nervous System:

Your brain, spinal cord, and nerves help control the muscle movements in the digestive tract to keep food moving. Your nervous system also helps with the release of enzymes that break food down, and it sends a signal to the brain when it is time to release waste.

Skeletal System:

Our teeth are part of our skeletal system—as are the rest of our bones. The jaw bone also plays a role in helping with digestion as it helps us chew. The lower jaw bone is the only bone in the skull that moves.

Urinary System:

After nutrients are absorbed into the blood through the digestive system and used by the body, the urinary system filters the bloodstream for any waste products and releases them as urine.

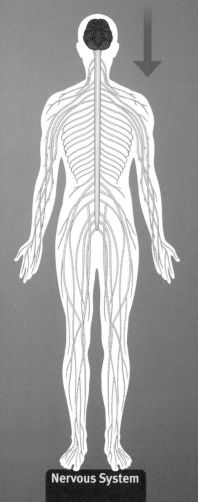

Nervous System

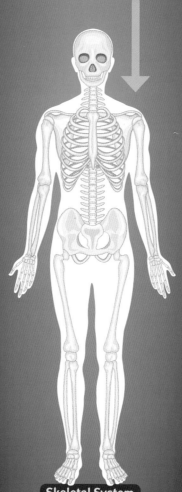

Skeletal System

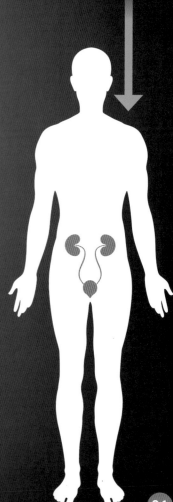

Urinary System

When you eat, your stomach can stretch up to five times bigger than when it is empty.

Overeating can cause a stomachache.

4

Ouch! My Stomach Hurts

Everyone has a stomachache at one time or another. But not every stomachache feels the same. Sometimes a person can eat too much at once. When that happens, the stomach distends beyond its usual limits and pushes against other organs. It makes us feel sluggish or just stuffed. Sometimes a stomachache can feel like a sharp pain—or an urgent need to use the bathroom. These problems are not uncommon. And they are just a few of the sicknesses that can affect our digestive system.

Some foods, like beef and chicken, have to be thoroughly cooked to avoid the risk of food poisoning.

Watch What You Eat!

Food poisoning can happen when a person eats something that contains harmful bacteria or viruses. That can cause cramps or a loss of appetite. The body will usually find a way to get rid of the food that is making it sick. Vomiting forces the food out of the mouth. Diarrhea, or loose poop, forces it out the other end. It is important to drink lots of fluids to replace all the liquids lost through vomiting and diarrhea.

What's That Noise?

Our bodies make lots of different noises. A few of them are caused by our digestive system! Sometimes we burp, sometimes we pass gas, and sometimes our stomachs rumble. One reason that happens is because when we eat and drink, we swallow air along with our food and drinks. When air ends up in our stomachs and needs to get out, it will often come out as a burp. Air that gets into our intestines comes out the other end! That rumbly sound our stomachs make is actually the sound of our intestines pushing air and food along. We don't hear it as much when we are full because the food covers up the sound.

Food Intolerances

Intolerances happen when the body has a hard time digesting a certain type of food. It can cause gas, **bloating**, and even stomach pain. One common food intolerance is lactose intolerance. Lactose is a sugar found in milk. Someone who is lactose intolerant will get a stomachache if they drink milk or eat dairy products.

Ice cream is a dairy product. So are cheese and yogurt.

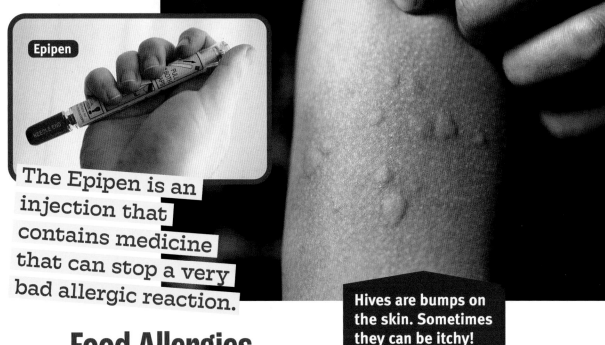

The Epipen is an injection that contains medicine that can stop a very bad allergic reaction.

Hives are bumps on the skin. Sometimes they can be itchy!

Food Allergies

Food allergies are different from food intolerances because they involve the immune system. With a food allergy, the immune system mistakenly identifies the food as something harmful and responds by releasing antibodies. Some food allergies might cause a rash or hives. Other food allergies cause similar symptoms to food poisoning. A severe allergic reaction can make it hard to breathe. Common food allergies are shellfish, eggs, peanuts, and tree nuts such as walnuts.

Kids throw up more easily—and more frequently—than adults.

Norovirus is a highly contagious stomach flu. A low-grade fever can be one of the symptoms.

Stomach Viruses

A virus, also known as the stomach flu, can cause stomach cramping and pain, vomiting, and diarrhea. Sometimes it might cause a fever, too. The stomach flu spreads through dirty water. It can also be spread from one person to another. It takes a few days for this virus to make its way through the digestive system. Drinking lots of water is important because it replaces fluids lost through diarrhea and vomiting. It also helps flush the virus out of the body.

A Busy System

There's not too much thought involved when we eat, except maybe thinking of how delicious our food is or if it's hot or cold. But while we're enjoying a meal, and also after, our digestive system is hard at work. Next time you take a bite of an apple or a slice of pizza, think about the process that starts with that first chomp. It's an amazing journey!

Apples are high in fiber, which is good for your digestive system!

Digestive Care

Doctors, nurses, and other providers work with us to prevent and treat disease. Here are a few healthcare professionals who treat the digestive system, and some of the tests they may perform.

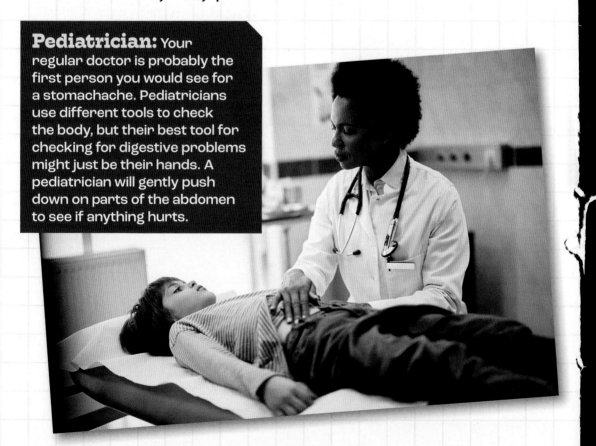

Pediatrician: Your regular doctor is probably the first person you would see for a stomachache. Pediatricians use different tools to check the body, but their best tool for checking for digestive problems might just be their hands. A pediatrician will gently push down on parts of the abdomen to see if anything hurts.

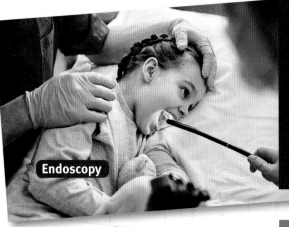
Endoscopy

Gastroenterologist: A gastroenterologist [ga-stroh-en-tuh-RAH-luh-jist] specializes in treating the digestive system. They use a tiny camera attached to a hose-like tool called a scope to see inside different parts of the digestive system. An upper endoscopy is done to examine the esophagus. A colonoscopy is done to look into the large intestine.

Allergy test

Allergist: This doctor can test for food allergies and will say which foods to stay away from. One of the first tools they use to test for allergies is a skin prick test. A number of **allergens** are put on the skin. If a person has an allergy to something, the skin will react with a raised red spot a few minutes later. An allergist can provide medicine that can help make an allergic reaction less severe.

Good food choices

Registered Dietitian: This person specializes in food and nutrition. They might work in a doctor's office, a hospital, or on their own in a private office. Registered dietitians help people make good food choices based on their health. Dietitians can help patients with food allergies or digestive issues, among other problems.

Take Care of Your Digestive System

Keeping your digestive system healthy is important. And if you take care of it now, you will have a healthier future. Here are four things you can do to protect your digestive health.

Eat a Healthy Diet

Make sure you follow a balanced diet. It should be rich in nutrients and include lots of fiber! Fiber helps keep your poop bulky and soft so it's easy to release when you have to go. It also feeds the good bacteria in your gut. Fiber is found in whole grains and many fruits and vegetables, especially leafy greens. Fiber is also found in beans.

Drink Plenty of Water

Water helps break down food so your body can extract more nutrients. It also prevents constipation. If there is not enough water in your body, more will be pulled from your poop. That will make it very hard to go to the bathroom. On average, kids over age eight should drink at least eight cups of water a day.

Exercise

Exercise increases your heart rate, which moves more blood throughout your body. That helps your digestive muscles move food along. Scientists also think exercise helps produce good bacteria in the gut. Being active for one hour a day is a great goal. You can play a sport, take a walk, or just run around with friends!

Get Enough Sleep

While you sleep, the digestive system grows new tissues and repairs existing tissues that have been working hard throughout the day. Sleeping also gives the digestive system time to slow down after hours of moving food from one place to the next.

Amount of saliva the average person makes in a day: 4 cups

Number of times the average person passes gas per day: 10 to 20

Amount of food the stomach can hold at one time: about 1 quart (0.9 liters)

Surface area of the small intestine if it was all spread out: 2,700 square feet (251 sq m)—just over half the size of a basketball court

Average amount of water the colon absorbs each day: 1 quart (.9 l)

Amount of time Americans over the age of 15 spend eating per day: 67 minutes

Did you find the truth?

F Rumbling is our stomach's way of telling us we're hungry.

T The small intestine is longer than the large intestine.

Resources

Other books in this series:

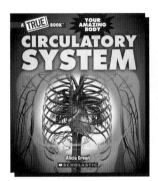 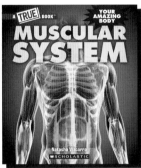 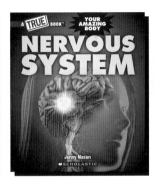 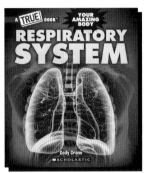

You can also look at:

Johnson, Rebecca L. *Your Digestive System*. Minneapolis, MN: Lerner, 2012.

Manolis, Kay. *The Digestive System*. Minneapolis, MN: Bellwether Media, 2009.

Pettiford, Rebecca. *The Digestive System*. Minneapolis, MN: Bellwether Media, 2019.

Taylor-Butler, Christine. *The Digestive System*. NY: Scholastic, 2008.

Glossary

abdomen (AB-duh-muhn) the front part of your body between your chest and hips

absorbed (ab-ZORBD) soaked up or taken in

allergen (AL-ur-juhn) a substance that causes an allergic reaction in someone

bacteria (bak-TEER-ee-uh) microscopic, single-celled living things that exist everywhere and that can either be useful or harmful

bloating (BLOH-ting) swelling from fluid or gas, often as a result of overeating

blood vessels (BLUHD VES-uhlz) any of the tubes in your body through which blood flows

contract (kuhn-TRAKT) become smaller

converted (kuhn-VUR-ted) turned into something else

enzymes (EN-zimes) proteins produced by a plant or an animal that cause chemical reactions to occur inside

immune system (i-MYOON SIS-tuhm) the system that protects your body against disease and infection

organs (OR-guhnz) parts of the body, such as the heart or the kidneys, that have a certain purpose

reflex (REE-fleks) an automatic action or movement that happens without a person's control or effort

Index

Page numbers in **bold** indicate illustrations.

About the Author

Priyanka Lamichhane spent 15 years with National Geographic Kids, where she led the reference publishing program and specialized in ideation, content development, editing, and project management. From encyclopedias to guidebooks and atlases to fact books, Priyanka has created hundreds of engaging titles on numerous topics for kids from preschool through middle grade. Most recently, Priyanka has been working with content producers and publishers, using her talents to create engaging books, articles, and activities for children. She loves learning about a wide variety of topics and shares the many fun facts floating around in her head with her three curious kids.